Love, Light, and Joy

Love, Light, and Joy

A 90 Day Practice That *Will* Change Your Life

By Brian A. Reekers

Love, Light, and Joy

A 90 Day Practice That *Will* Change Your Life

ISBN: 0615626904
ISBN-13: 978-0615626901

This book is dedicated with Gratitude and Appreciation to God and the Angels who brought this book into being.

Table of Contents

Preface

What follows is a Divinely Inspired message as delivered from The Angelic Realm. It is a three phase practice, or system which, when followed as suggested, will open you up to a new way of experiencing life in the physical realm. You will also notice, as you integrate and apply these techniques, that as your experience of life changes so the world around you will change as well. This "ripple effect" is instrumental in the healing of humanity and the world.

With Blessings and Love,

Brian

Phase I

Feel The Love

Greetings, Dear One, and welcome.

We are elated and overjoyed that you have found your way here and that you are open to receiving this message as a means of improving the quality of your life as you inhabit your earthly vessels. We are delighted to share these thoughts and techniques with you in order that you may begin your journey to a life filled with Peace and Love.

This program is designed to be followed and applied to your life over a ninety day period. However, it is essential that during the first 30 days you commit yourself only to this first Phase. For in that time this practice will become second-nature to you and thus provide a solid foundation for the lessons that will follow in the second and third Phases.

The first Phase of the program is all about Love. Love is the basis of all Creation. All that exists is the result of Love. Love is the energy that binds the Universe in place. It is the energy that binds the atoms together as they join to create everything that exists in your physical world. Love is the basis of virtually every belief system which exists in your world. Love creates. Just as the Creator's Love brought all being into existence, so that Love continues to create as it flows through the physical world. Art, music, literature; all are the product of Love. Love permeates, penetrates, and procreates. Love flows as ceaselessly as a river. Love is as boundless as the wind.

The Love of which we speak is unconditional. This Love holds no judgment. This Love is all-forgiving, ever-patient, and ever-present. This is Love in its truest form.

Before you can use Love to change the world, or anyone or anything in it, you must first develop and cultivate this Love within and for your self. For you cannot share with another that which you do not possess, both within, and for, your self. This is the task at hand.

At this point there are some of you thinking "But I already love myself." This is true for all of you as evidenced by the fact that you take time each day to care for yourselves. You clothe, cleanse, nourish, and house your physical bodies. This is true and such behavior does exhibit self-love to a certain degree. However, those practices truly are more evident of your survival instinct.

The true gauge of sincere self-love can be measured by observing the way you treat others as well as the manner in which you treat yourselves. Consider the following questions:

Do you ever find yourself being critical?

Do you ever belittle people?

Do you sit in judgment?

3

Do you ever feel fearful?

Are there things about yourself you would like to change?

Are there things about others you would like to change?

Have you ever felt that you weren't good enough or that you didn't measure up?

Have you ever cast blame?

Have you ever caused harm, either to yourself or another?

If you answered "yes," or even "maybe" to any of these questions then this program is for you.

If you are uncertain or have any doubt then take time over the next 24 hours to truly pay attention to how you talk to your self and others. Pay attention to how you treat your self and those around you. Look closely. You may be surprised by what you discover.

The first step in the process is to understand and accept that everything and everyone you encounter in life is there for the sole purpose of helping you to grow and evolve. Every relationship, including your relationship with your self, is designed to teach you that which you are ready to learn. Listen and pay close attention to your reaction to these encounters. More than likely this will be an eye-opening experience.

Have you ever listened, really listened, to the way you speak to your self? Are your words kind and loving or critical and harsh? Do you offer your self praise and kudos or are you demeaning and debasing? Mind you, these un-loving words don't necessarily have to be overtly vicious and condescending. Sometimes, and maybe more often than not, these un-loving examples may be quite subtle. Simple statements may appear to be innocent enough but consider their effects. Especially if they are repeated time and time again. For example, while dressing to go out you look into the mirror and say to

5

your self, "This makes me look fat." Our first question to you is would you say "That makes you look fat" to a complete stranger? Most likely you would not unless, of course, you were just being cruel. Well then, how cruel is it to say that to your self? How long before you alter the statement to simply say "I am fat?" How loving and kind is that? Another aspect of this same example is this; would you want someone else to speak to you in this manner? Probably not.

Another example to consider; in scripture is the story of a group of people who came to Jesus wishing to stone an adulteress. When asked what they should do Jesus' reply was simply that whosoever was without sin should cast the first stone, which caused the crowd to disperse. Consider this from the perspective of judgment. If you are in judgment of another you are, in fact, in judgment of your self. In truth, when you feel the need to judge someone, or their actions, it is merely because they have reflected to you some judgment you hold about your self. Think carefully and honestly about this and you will discover its truth, even though it may not be comfortable or immediately apparent.

One last example; while driving to work someone cuts you off in traffic. You immediately feel yourself get enraged and possibly you say some unkind words or make an unkind gesture. While you may feel better by the time you arrive at your destination you may well find yourself retelling the event to anyone who will listen. With each telling you feel the same emotions well up inside you. By the end of the day you feel exhausted and irritated for reasons you can't explain. This is an example of giving away your power.

Each of these examples, as well as many more, can be avoided or overcome by simply implementing the practice we are about to share. It is important to remember that this practice is designed to take place over a thirty day period in order to gain the maximum benefit and to instill itself into your inner-being. This will also serve to establish the foundation for the Phases yet to follow, each being designed as a thirty day practice as well.

.

Internalizing Love

The Practice

It is important to spend at least 20 minutes a day focused on this practice. While you can combine this with other activities such as walking it is our highest recommendation that this be a separate dedicated practice. While the 20 minutes can be broken up throughout your day we highly suggest a continuous 20 minute practice for maximum benefit. Repeating the phrases throughout your day, however, will serve to increase the benefits and amplify your results.

While this is a very simple practice it is also a very powerful practice. By entering into a relaxed state and repeating these phrases as prescribed you will establish a deep and powerful relationship with the Love Energy. By connecting with this Energy on an intimate level you will change the way in which you

8

relate not only to your self but to the world around you. As you deepen your connection with the Energy of Love you will notice changes taking place in your relationship to your self and others, as well as a shift in your perception and experience of life. As this shift occurs others will take note of these changes. Watch the world through child-like eyes and you will be amazed by the miracles which surround you.

Enjoy and be well.

With Divine Love,

The Angels

Internalizing Love

Days 1 through 10

Begin by finding a comfortable place where you will not be disturbed or suffer any kind of interruption. Be certain to wear comfortable clothing that will not restrict your breathing.

Once you are situated start by taking a few nice, deep cleansing breaths. See yourself surrounded by a brilliant white light, as though you are encased within a bubble. This is the Divine Light of Love and Protection. As you continue to breathe deeply and slowly, imagine this light flowing into your body each time you inhale. As you exhale see this light removing any tension or anxiety you may be holding. Also, allow this light to remove any negative thoughts, feelings, and emotions as well as any negative energy you may be holding or have accumulated. As you continue with this portion of the exercise you will notice that the light begins to flow in and out with equal brilliance. When you are at this point you are ready to begin.

As you inhale mentally say the phrase "I Love You."

As you exhale mentally repeat the phrase "I Love You."

Do not worry about where, or to whom, this thought is being directed. Simply continue to say "I Love You" each time you inhale and exhale. This will bring you into the space of giving and receiving Love freely and easily. This begins the process of internalizing Love.

Internalizing Love

Days 11 through 20

The preparation for days 11 through 20 is the same as days 1 through 10. Find a comfortable place where you won't be disturbed and wear comfortable clothing so as not to restrict your breathing. Surround yourself with the Divine White Light of Love and Protection and allow this light to fill and cleanse you of all tension and negativity. Breathe slowly and deeply until you feel sufficiently cleansed and relaxed.

As you inhale mentally say the phrase "I Am Love."

As you exhale mentally repeat the phrase "I Am Love" as well.

This section is all about coming to know and accept that you are a Creation of Love. Specifically, this is about knowing that you are the embodiment of Divine Love. If this feels uncomfortable just remember to be kind and gentle with your self. Trust us, this will get easier. Be persistent and allow any emotions that come up to be released into the Light that surrounds you. For added benefit, repeat this phrase often throughout the day.

Internalizing Love

Days 21 through 30

Once again the preparation is the same as before. Get comfortable, surround yourself in the Divine Light and, as you breathe deeply and slowly, allow this light to fill and cleanse you. Once you feel sufficiently relaxed and free of negativity you are ready to begin.

As you inhale mentally say the phrase "I Love You."

As you exhale mentally say the phrase "I Am Love."

During this final section of Phase I is where you truly express and internalize Divine Love. As you say "I Love You," see your self as the recipient of the sentiment. Say "I Love You" to every cell and atom of your being. Say it with sincerity. Feel its energy as it permeates every part of your being.

As you say "I AM Love" you are embracing the Power and Truth of who you are. Make this statement with feeling and confidence. Declare this as your Truth, for it is surely God's Truth.

"God is Love, and he who abides in Love abides in God, and God in him." (1 John 4:16)

Phase II

See The Light

Greetings, Dear One, and welcome to Phase II.

We are delighted and overjoyed by your decision to continue with this work. We know that you have begun to experience changes based on the work you have completed in Phase I. We know that your experience of these changes may, in some cases, be quite subtle at first but that you are experiencing changes, nonetheless.

In Phase II of this practice we are going to be concentrating on the energy of Light. The Light of which we speak is that Inner Light that shines through you. As you begin to develop this energy within your self you will begin to radiate this Light, thus affecting the people, places, and situations around you. You will begin to experience a feeling of lightness (no pun intended) as well. Others will notice this radiance in you. You may begin to hear adjectives such as "glowing" or "shining" or "beaming" being used to describe you. Those gifted with vision may notice a change in your aura, the light energy which surrounds you. Whatever the case may be, you will shine brighter, and feel more connected, by the end of this second Phase. Additionally, you will begin to notice this same Light in the people you encounter.

So what is this Light of which we speak? Simply put, it is the Light of God which exists in all creation. It is that Divine Spark that brings life to All That Is. It is God within you.

Just as everything in existence is part of God, so then a part of God lives within everything that exists. This part, or piece, of God is evidenced as Light. This Light of God, or Spark, resides within each and every person of Earth. To be truthful, this Light resides within everything on Earth; animal, vegetable, and mineral.

Much has been written about this Light. "This little Light of mine, I'm gonna let it shine." "I am the Light of the world." "Let there be Light." These are but a few examples. Even in reference to the physical lies reference to the Light of God.

So then, how does focusing on this Light within begin to change your experience of Life and the world around you? To answer this question we must go back to the beginning or back to basics.

As discussed in our previous lesson, you cannot give to another that which you don't truly possess with regard to your self. Without truly holding Love in your heart for your self you cannot truly give Love to anyone else. By now you should be well on your way to firmly establishing the Self-Love of which we spoke. In so doing you should begin to notice that Love flows from you more freely than before. And, as Love flows from you, it cannot help but to return to you even greater than before.

The same holds true with regard to "seeing" things in others. You cannot see clearly that which resides in someone else unless you can clearly see that same thing residing in your self. In other words, you cannot recognize that which you don't possess. It is only by seeing, or recognizing, or realizing, or honoring, or connecting with this Light, or Spark, within your own soul will you then be able to see, recognize, realize, honor, and connect with this Light, or Spark, within another. Only by knowing God within your self can you truly know God within your neighbor. Only by knowing God within your self will you know God within All Creation.

Therefore, this next section of the Practice is all about developing that connection to the Light of God that exists within you. And so, let us begin.

Internalizing Light

The Practice

By the end of this Phase of the Practice you will know that the Light of God exists in you as well as in everyone you encounter. You will acknowledge this Light's presence in your self as well as them. By knowing this Light as it exists in you, and by knowing this Light as it exists in those around you, as well as in all creation, you will now begin to experience the Oneness of All Creation. You will now grow in the understanding that while everything and everyone may appear to be separate, all are in fact one within, and all are connected by the Light of God. So in the way in which you treat your self you treat the world around you. So in the way in which you treat the world around you, you treat your self. Consider this always.

With Divine Light,

The Angels

Internalizing Light

Days 31- 40

By now you have already established your Sacred Space in which to practice. Most likely you are also versed in surrounding and cleansing yourself with Divine Light as you breathe deeply and slowly. Once you are comfortable and centered you may begin.

As you inhale mentally say the phrase "The Light of God..."

As you exhale complete the statement "...is within me now."

This part of the process is about accepting that the Light of God is already within you and is part of you. This is about bringing this "knowingness" into your heart and mind. This is about realizing your own Divinity as being One with God.

Bear in mind that it is acceptable to substitute another term for "God" if that term makes you uncomfortable. For example, "The Light of Creation..." or "The Light of Source..." is an acceptable substitute. Be consistent in whatever term you use. The important thing is to realize that this Light already exists within your soul.

Internalizing Light

Days 41-50

Again, follow your opening procedure. Get quiet. Get comfortable. Breathe deeply and slowly. See the Divine Light surrounding, protecting, filling, and cleansing you. When you feel balanced you may begin.

As you inhale mentally say the phrase "As I Am Light..."

As you exhale complete the statement "...so All Are Light."

This section is about coming to the understanding that All Creation is of One Spirit. This is about realizing that separation is but an illusion. The Light that exists within you exists in All That Is. As you are filled with the Light that is God, so everything and everyone in existence is filled with the same Light. As you are the Light, so all you see is the Light.

Internalizing Light

Days 51-60

Get comfortable. Get centered. Surround, fill, and protect yourself with Divine Light as you breathe deeply and easily. When you are ready, begin.

As you inhale mentally say the phrase "I Am One with God."

As you exhale mentally say the phrase "God Is One with Me."

Though this may seem difficult and uncomfortable to speak, stay the course. For this is the Divine Truth, that as you are within God, so God is within you. As you are One with God, so God is One with You. Claim this knowledge, this Truth, as your own.

Again, you may substitute a different term for "God" if you would feel more comfortable. Our only caution in so doing is to be consistent. If possible use the same substitution as in the previous portion of this exercise.

Phase III

Feel The Joy

Greetings, Dear One, and welcome to Phase III.

Now that you have completed Phases I and II you are no doubt beginning to experience a shift in the way in which you experience life and perceive the world around you. You are now aware of the Divine Love which flows to you and through you. You are, most likely, feeling a greater and truer Love for your self and the world around you. The Love you have for your self you now have for others.

You should also be experiencing the presence of the Light of God within your self and everyone around you. You now have an understanding that God is present in, and part of, everyone and everything. This includes you, too.

Give Thanks and Praise, for this is truly miraculous to be experiencing this transition, no matter how great or how faint it may feel. You are truly experiencing a transition in your life.

So, Dear One, we now come to Phase III of this Practice. This Phase is all about Joy.

Joy is your natural state of being. Joy is the product of Living Love. Joy is the result of Living in the Light. In short, Love + Light = Joy.

When All was created it was done from Love and filled with Joy. It is God's intent that all experience life joyously. Sadly, most have forgotten what Joy is and how to experience it. We say "forgotten" for that is the Truth of things.

When you first came into a physical body your natural state was one of Joy. Your Spirit was filled with Joy at the prospect of this new adventure. To validate this

Truth simply take the time to observe infants, puppies, kittens, etc. These new beings exist in Joy. It radiates from them with such power that it directly touches the hearts of all who come in contact with them. This is the perfect example of the Power and Presence of Joy.

Over time this Heavenly Joy can be lost, buried, or simply forgotten. This can be the result of environment, experiences, teachings, trainings, or any number of influences. Regardless of how it has been forgotten, it is important for you to know that it still exists within you and that you are able to reconnect with it. Once you remember and reconnect, your Joy will then flow through you with Great Power, influencing and affecting the lives of others and serving to raise the vibration of the world as a whole. For Joy is a powerful healing energy.

Internalizing Joy

The Practice

By the completion of Phase III you will begin to have a more Joyful experience of life. More will appear in your life to bring you Joy. Joy will flow through you and thus influence the world around you. Your Spirit will feel lighter and brighter with each new day.

With Divine Joy,

The Angels

Internalizing Joy

Days 61 – 70

We begin as always by surrounding yourself in God's Divine White Light of Love and Protection. Breathe gently and deeply, allowing this Light to fill and cleanse you in Body, Heart, Mind, and Spirit. Release any low vibration thoughts, energies, and emotions into the Light to be removed and healed.

Once you feel centered, clear, and calm focus on taking slow, gentle breaths.

As you inhale mentally say the phrase "Joy is natural..."

As you exhale complete the statement "...And comes easily to me."

This section is simply about remembering. It is about remembering that Joy is a natural state of being. It is about remembering that Joy is meant to flow freely and easily. It is about remembering that you already possess Joy and that you deserve to be Joyful.

Internalizing Joy

Days 71 – 80

Again, take time to surround and fill yourself with Protective Light, center yourself in your Heart, and cleanse yourself of any low vibration energy. Breathe easily and steadily.

As you inhale mentally say the phrase "I Am filled with Joy."

As you exhale mentally say the phrase "Joy flows through me to the World."

Here is where you invite Joy into your heart. Joy fills you and lives in you. This is also where you become an instrument of Joy. Share the Joy that fills you freely and lovingly with the entire world. Joy, like a smile, is contagious

.

Internalizing Joy

Days 81 – 90

We begin, as always, by surrounding, filling, and cleansing yourself with Divine Light and Love. Release all negativity and low vibration energy. Establish a pattern of steady, gentle breathing.

As you inhale mentally say the phrase "I live Joy..."

As you exhale complete the statement "...for I AM Joy."

Claim your Power and your Truth. Be Love! Be Light! Be Joy! Share the Joy that is now in you with everyone you meet. What you give freely and with Love will be returned to you one hundred fold. So be Joyous, always!

What's Next?

If you have come this far and completed this 90 Day Practice, then your life will have changed, becoming richer, fuller, lighter, and more peaceful and fulfilling. But it doesn't end here, for this is only the beginning.

During this 90 Day Practice you have internalized Love, Light, and Joy. In addition, you have developed a Daily Spiritual Practice. It is our sincere hope and prayer that you continue with this practice, for in so doing you will benefit greatly.

In continuing this practice you can begin again and repeat the entire process. You may want to repeat a single Phase if you feel you require more emphasis in a particular area. Or you can utilize this structure to incorporate new ideals, or energies, into your life.

Use this practice to internalize Gratitude, Appreciation, Peace, or any number of high vibrations. If you need help with phrasing for a particular vibration simply call on us Angels and we will bring the necessary guidance into your heart.

You may simply want to take 10 to 30 days to simply focus on your breathing to quiet your mind.

The key is to continue.

With Great Blessings of Divine Love, Light, and Joy,

The Angels

About the Author

Brian A. Reekers is "The Angel Guy." He has been communicating with the Angels and the Angelic Realm since 2001. Prior to that, he had led an ordinary life with jobs ranging from dishwasher to delivery, busboy to bartender, and a more than 25 year career in real estate and related industries. However, it was in 2001 that he underwent an awakening and began to walk his Spiritual path in earnest. The most significant aspect of this was *remembering* how to hear the voices of the Angels. Since that time Brian has devoted himself to receiving and delivering the Angels' messages in order to help others improve their lives, recognize their Divinity, and strengthen their connection to the Divine.